DRAFTING A NEW STRATEGY FOR PUBLIC DIPLOMACY AND STRATEGIC COMMUNICATION

by

Colonel Timothy J. Loney
United States Army

Dr. Anna T. Waggener
Project Adviser

U.S. Army War College
CARLISLE BARRACKS, PENNSYLVANIA 17013

ABSTRACT

AUTHOR: Colonel Timothy J. Loney

TITLE: Drafting a New Strategy for Public Diplomacy and Strategic Communication

FORMAT: Strategy Research Project

DATE: 9 March 2009   WORD COUNT: 5,014   PAGES: 26

KEY TERMS: Information Operation, National Security Strategy

CLASSIFICATION: Unclassified

In May 2007, the United States Government published its *U.S. National Strategy for Public Diplomacy and Strategic Communication*. The strategy, authored by the Policy Coordinating Committee (PCC) on Public Diplomacy and Strategic Communication, is the first attempt at coordinating Strategic Communication efforts across the interagency community. Although a good start, the current strategy is preoccupied with the war on terror, presents a miss match in mission and objectives, fails to recognize key strategic audiences, and accepts an adversarial relationship with the media.

This Strategy Research Project (SRP) paper reviews the current *Strategy* in terms of ends, ways, and means and in terms of its suitability, feasibility and acceptability and provides recommendations for drafting the new *U.S. National Strategy for Public Diplomacy and Strategic Communication*.

DRAFTING A NEW STRATEGY FOR PUBLIC DIPLOMACY AND STRATEGIC COMMUNICATION

Over the past seven years, the war on terror has dominated U.S. foreign policy. Evidence of this preoccupation is found throughout *The National Security Strategy of the United States of America* in which former President George W. Bush's endorsement opened with, "America is at war."[1] This pointed endorsement and the document's preoccupation with the war on terror conjure images of total war. Yet this image is inconsistent with the mood of the country. For most Americans, the wars in Iraq and Afghanistan have little impact on their daily lives and they favor withdrawing from Iraq within a year regardless of the situation.[2]

This inconsistency between the former President's message and the American people's perception has resulted from either the government's inability to communicate reality or from an overzealous message that focuses too much attention on a relatively small issue. This contradiction in conjunction with President Barack Obama's emphasis on rebuilding alliances and meeting with all nations to advance American interests will require the Obama administration to take a closer look at the nation's public diplomacy and strategic communication strategy.[3] The reasons are clear. As a new administration seeks a more participative role in international affairs, it will need to implement a foreign policy consistent with this position and develop a strategy for delivering clear and compelling messages in order to maintain support at home and abroad. To maximize this effort, the administration will need to reexamine the *U.S. National Strategy for Public Diplomacy and Strategic Communication.*

Issue

Early in the new administration's tenure, President Obama will need to rewrite the *U.S. National Strategy for Public Diplomacy and Strategic Communication*. This new strategy should reflect changes the new administration hopes to implement, identify and provide guidance to those who will play an active role, and offer assurance to both domestic and international audiences.

Background

In January 2008, the *Defense Science Board Task Force on Strategic Communication* released its third report in a decade on strategic communication. The 2008 report stated that, "progress has been made in improving the nation's strategic communication capability [with] …establishing strategic communication as a priority at the highest levels of the U.S. government" [4] as the most significant of these improvements.

The report also highlighted the establishment of the Policy Coordinating Committee (PCC) on Public Diplomacy and Strategic Communication that was established in April 2006. In May of 2007, this PCC released a *U.S. National Strategy for Public Diplomacy and Strategic Communication*.[5] The 2008 DSB report claimed, "This document presents a clear and well-articulated strategy intended to serve as a framework for strategic communication implementation plans across the interagency."[6]

Purpose

This paper reviews the current *U.S. National Strategy for Public Diplomacy and Strategic Communication* dated May 2007 in terms of Arthur F. Lykke, Jr.'s Army War College strategy model of ends, ways, and means. In his article, *Towards A Theory of*

Strategy: Art Lykke and the Army War College Strategy Model, Harry R. Yarger defined Ends (objectives) as "what is to be accomplished."[7] He held that, "Ends are objectives that if accomplished create, or contribute to, the achievement of the desired end state ..."[8]

Yarger also stated that ways, "explain how the ends are to be accomplished by the employment of resources."[9] He said that, "The concept must be explicit enough to provide planning guidance to those who must implement and resource it."[10] Means are the resources used to accomplish the ends or objectives. This paper examines the current communcation strategy in terms of ends, ways and means of the construct and provides recommendations for drafting the new strategy.

This paper also examines the current strategy in terms of the suitability, feasibility and acceptability of the approach and provides recommendations for drafting the new strategy. This construct is often used by strategists to evaluate a strategy during development by answering the following questions.

> Suitability--will its attainment accomplish the effect desired (relates to objective)?

> Feasibility--can the action be accomplished by the means available (relates to concept)?

> Acceptability--are the consequences of cost justified by the importance of the effect desired (relates to resources/concept)?[11]

For clarity, this paper limits its discussion to the *U.S. National Strategy for Public Diplomacy and Strategic Communication* document. Both the Bush and Obama administrations' policies are not debated but sometimes used to illustrate specific public diplomacy and strategic communication points. In illustrating these points, it is assumed that the policies themselves are acceptable. In this way, discussions focus on the current and recommended new public diplomacy and strategic communication strategy, not the policies the strategies promote.

Ends, Observations, and Recommendations

In May 2007, the United States Government published its first *U.S. National Strategy for Public Diplomacy and Strategic Communication*. This new document identified three strategic objectives (ends) to guide the public diplomacy and strategic communication strategy:

> 1) America must offer a positive vision of hope and opportunity that is rooted in our most basic values. 2) With our partners, we seek to isolate and marginalize violent extremists who threaten the freedom and peace sought by civilized people of every nation, culture and faith. 3) America must work to nurture common interests and values between Americans and peoples of different countries, cultures and faiths across the world.[12]

There are three problems with these objectives that should be considered when developing the new strategy. First, by definition, an objective is a "...clearly defined, decisive, and attainable goal..."[13] or in other words, an aim to be achieved. These objectives however, appear to describe activities or how to do something (ways) rather than a goal or objective (ends). All three stated objectives contain action verbs. The first objective, "America must offer a positive vision..." contains an action verb "offer." The second objective, "...we seek to isolate and marginalize violent..." contains the verbs "isolate and marginalize," while the third objective, "America must work to nurture common interests..." also contains an action verb "work." This wording creates confusion when trying to decide what the U.S. is trying to achieve.

The first objective could be interpreted that the United States is more concerned with the "offering" than the actual awareness of basic United States values. The second objective could be interpreted as more concerned with trying to "isolate and marginalize" than with the outcome these activities are hoping to produce. The third objective could be interpreted that the United States should "nurture common interests and values" [14] simply for the sake of nurturing common interests and values.

In addition to unclear guidance, equally problematic is defining success in obtaining these objectives. For example, the first objective could infer that the United States does not offer "a positive vision of hope and opportunity" and therefore success could be interpreted as now offering the vision without regard to whether it is received.

The second problem with the stated objectives is that the *U.S. National Strategy for Public Diplomacy and Strategic Communication* is preoccupied with the war on terror. The strategy provides more than two pages of core messages focused on the war on terror and only three quarters of a page for the remaining information. This preoccupation with the war is also reflected in the document's stated objectives in which one of the three objectives specifically addresses this issue.

The results of the 2009 presidential election and current polling data confirm that Americans are overwhelmingly focused on economic and domestic issues, not the war on terror. During the past election, Senator John McCain emphasized his experience in foreign policy issues and was widely recognized as the stronger candidate in this area, yet lost the election to Senator Barack Obama. Recent polls confirm that most respondents viewed the economy (93%) and the war in Iraq (84%) as either "extremely important" or "very important" when asked, "Which of the following should be Barack Obama's top priority as president: the economy, health care, the situations in Iraq and Afghanistan, energy, the federal budget deficit, or something else?" Only eleven percent chose the situations in Iraq and Afghanistan. [15]

The third problem is that the current strategy's list of objectives fails to include desired outcomes for friends, coalition partners, allies, and the United States domestic audiences. These omissions seem to assume that these groups either fully support the administration's views or the groups' opinions simply do not matter, when, in fact, the opposite is true. Arguably, these audiences are the most important and must be included to support U.S. intrests abroad.

Internationally, the United State's friends, coalition partners, and allies provide advice, legitimacy, and support within the international community. However, disturbing trends indicate that these traditional friends, coalition partners, and allies' resolve to support the United States maybe eroding.

> ...in 2002, 64% of Europeans viewed U.S. leadership in world affairs as "desirable," and 31% as "undesirable," these proportions reversed by 2004 and have remained virtually constant since then. In 2008, 36% of Europeans viewed U.S. leadership in world affairs as "desirable" and 59% viewed it as "undesirable.[16]

This overwhelming "undesirable" view of U.S. leadership undermines the ability of the United States to achieve its international goals. As Joseph S. Nye, Jr., points out in his (2004) article *The Decline of America's Soft Power*, "When the United States becomes so unpopular that being pro-American is a kiss of death in other countries' domestic politics, foreign political leaders are unlikely to make helpful concessions..."[17]

In order to reverse this trend and reestablish a positive view of U.S. leadership in world affairs, the United States must ensure that friends, coalition partners, and allies understand that it values their input on international affairs, will consider their position before acting, and remains steadfast in honoring all commitments. Unfortunately, this important task and these important audiences are missing from the current strategy's list of objectives and audiences.

Domestically, similar statistics indicate an overwhelming "disapproval" rating of the Bush administration's leadership. According to PollingReport.com, a website which consolidates polling data from other sources, President Bush's overall job approval rating ranged from 20% to 36% in 2008 while his disapproval rating ranged from 59% to 78% during the same year.

Assuming that the administration's policies are acceptable, then it is a lack of understanding these policies that is the primary cause for these results and an indicator of an ineffective strategic communication strategy. Simply accepting a low approval rating as an unavoidable hazard of making correct yet unpopular decisions will no longer be effective. Public support is necessary to reach long-term foreign policy goals while adversaries will continue to exploit this vulnerability in order to erode public support.

> As a democracy and representatives of the people, the United States Government must have the support of its citizens. Therefore, it has a responsibility to keep its domestic audience informed and, if necessary, explain unpopular actions. The objective of keeping the American people informed was omitted on the current strategy and needs to be included in the next communication strategy.

Ends - Audience, Observations and Recommendations

The current *U.S. National Strategy for Public Diplomacy and Strategic Communication* identifies three strategic audiences (key influencers, vulnerable populations, and mass audiences). Two of these audiences, like the objectives, are focused on the war on terror while the third is defined in terms of ways or how to reach large groups. The document describes "Key Influencers" as "...those whose views can have a ripple effect throughout society."[18] Further, it narrowly defines the purpose for engaging these key influencers as,"... [to] encourage and empower them to speak out against the forces of violent extremism and in favor of peaceful resolution of disputes, tolerance and freedom."[19] The strategy identifies subgroups (youth, women and girls, and minorities) within the second audience, vulnerable populations, because they are "…groups most vulnerable to extremist ideology.

The third strategic audience, mass audiences, acknowledges the reach of mass media including print, radio, and television, but fails to address to what end. It can be assumed that the purpose of the policy is to support the three stated objectives. However, as stated earlier, these objectives are narrowly focused and ambiguous.

Although difficult to detect by these broadly defined audiences yet noticeably absent when examining the actual policy are two extremely important audiences. Missing are the United States friends, coalition partners, and allies, as well as United States domestic. As discussed earlier, it is imperative that the scope of this strategy be expanded and more inclusive. Though difficult to support with facts, the lack of attention to these audiences in the current strategy may have contributed to fomer President Bush's poor approval rating within the United States, as well as erosion in approval of the United States leadership among traditional friends, coalition partners, and allies.

When rewriting the *U.S. National Strategy for Public Diplomacy and Strategic Communication* objective(s), the administration should clearly define the objectives as decisive and attainable goals and reduce the emphasis on the war on terror yet make them broad by addressing additional audiences. In order to provide clarity of purpose, audiences within the new *U.S. National Strategy for Public Diplomacy and Strategic Communication* should be defined within the stated objectives.

At a minimum, the new document should include objectives similar to: 1) International awareness of positive U.S. Government and nongovernment activities is increased. 2) Misinformation about the U.S. Government and nongovernment activities is minimized and marginalized. 3) U.S. friends, coalition partners, and allies are reassured of the United State's resolve to honor all commitments. 4) Those who would otherwise threaten peace and freedom are discouraged and fail to act. 5) National awareness of U.S. Government and nongovernment activities is increased. These objectives are clearly defined, are obtainable given the strategy's focus on public diplomacy and strategic communication (ways), are broad yet allow for supporting the war on terror, and include previously overlooked audiences.

If the new administration wants to address a specific audience because of its strategic importance, then it, like the objectives, should have at least one desired outcome. To promote the importance of North Atlantic Treaty Organization (NATO) as both a ways and a means for providing regional stability, then the new strategy should contain an objective that identifies NATO nations with a desired outcome. The objective could state, "NATO nations are reassured of the United State's resolve to honor NATO commitments and utilize the organization as a primary means of discussing and resolving international issues."

Ways – Actions or Activities, Observations and Recommendations

This paper focuses on four important components of "ways"; actions or activities, media interaction, themes and messages, and measuring success. In terms of actions or activities, the strategy establishes three public diplomacy priorities (expand education and exchange programs, modernize communications, and promote the "diplomacy of

9

deeds") and provides examples of other possible methods. The new administration should examine and develop priorities based on President Obama's preferences. For example, the President effectively leveraged the power of the internet during the election to highlight his position on the issues while discrediting his opponent's position. This same technique could be used to help keep the American people informed of policy decisions and activities while discrediting adversaries. It should be noted that these postings should not attack adversaries, a technique often used in political campaigns, but rather clarify positions and emphasize facts.

Ways – Media Interaction, Observations and Recommendations

The current communications strategy recognizes the importance of the media, but seems to treat it as a neutral source (ways) of getting information to select audiences. While this may have been true in the past, the relationship between the U.S. Government and the media has changed over the years and must be addressed in the new communication strategy.

The Bush administration's actual relationship with the media could be characterized as symbiotic, which always benefited the media while occasionally helping or sometimes hurting the administration. In his article, "Bad News," Richard A. Posner identified two trends that he attributed to the growth in the number of media outlets and competition for market share. The first trend was that competition "…has caused polarization, pushing the already liberal media farther left."[20] Second, "the news media have also become more sensational, more prone to scandal and possibly less accurate."[21] These trends hinder the ability of the administration to reach audiences with timely and accurate information. In some cases, they have caused the administration to

10

expend resources in order to discount misinformation. Posner provided two examples in his article which undoubtedly damaged the administration's reputation.

> ...the "60 Minutes II" broadcast in which Dan Rather paraded what were probably forged documents concerning George W. Bush's National Guard service, and to Newsweek's erroneous report, based on a single anonymous source, that an American interrogator had flushed a copy of the Koran down the toilet...[22]

Accusing the media of being liberal, sensational, and inaccurate in the nation's communication strategy would serve only to exacerbate the problem. The Obama administration should implement mitigating techniques (imbedding reporters, developing personal relationships, demanding a recant of misinformation, etc.) which will help to ensure more timely and accurate information.

Ways – Themes and Messages, Observations and Recommendations

The first observation is that the current strategy does not contain "themes," thus limiting it to "core messages." The U.S. Joint Forces Command, Commander's Handbook for Strategic Communication, makes a clear distinction between themes and messages. A theme is an overarching concept or intention, designed for broad application, while a message is a narrowly focused communication directed at a specific audience.[23] The strategy fails to provide overarching, national level themes that would establish a foundation for assisting the interagency community in developing their own themes and messages tailored for specific audiences. A lack of themes limits the interagency to simply repeating the strategy's provided messages, which may not resonate with their audience.

The new strategy must also encourage all segments of the United States Government in developing agency-specific plans to develop themes and messages.

Different government agencies naturally speak to different segments of the larger audiences and should develop tailored themes and messages that complement those in the National strategy yet resonate a deeper meaning with this segment. The Department of the Army could reach out to NATO partners, emphasizing the strong bond of the alliance in support of the third recommended objective U.S. friends, coalition partners, and allies would be reassured of the United State's resolve to honor all commitments.

The Obama administration must also understand that this document, *U.S. National Strategy for Public Diplomacy and Strategic Communication* is a "ways" of communicating and consider using a different tone. On the backdrop of the country's focus on the war on terror and the establishment of the new United States Africa Command (AFRICOM), many in the international community are concerned that the United States is using its military as the primary lead in international affairs. The current strategy uses military terminology and could be interpreted as another indicator of the militarization of U.S. foreign policy.

As evidence of this growing concern, General William E. "Kip" Ward, commander, AFRICOM, told representatives from 43 African nations during the U.S.-Africa Defense Policy Dialogue that, "I don't want to take over U.S. foreign policy," and stressed that U.S. civilian leaders make policy, not the military. The strategy should not add to the debate that the United States is militarizing its foreign policy.

The document uses the term "target audience" seven times and the expression "engage" several times to describe United States Government activities; "Identify and engage key influencers..." These terms have an aggressive militaristic overtone and

12

should be avoided in open source documents, especially in the country's strategy on diplomacy and strategic communication. Replacing the term "target audience" with "audience" and avoiding words like "engage" will soften the tone and make it less intrusive for those audiences.

Finally, the new strategy should highlight the lead for implementing foreign policy as the Department of State and that the Department of Defense activities are in direct support of the Department of State. Although this statement seems obvious and unnecessary, it would help to counter misconceptions of U.S. foreign policy. In addition, many of these "core messages" fail to follow generally accepted guidelines for crafting messages in that they should be clear and concise. One of the messages contains seven lines of text. To increase the probability that the interagency community will use these messages, that these messages will echo in the media and resonate in the intended audiences, they must be easily understood and easily repeated.

Ways – Measuring Success, Observations and Recommendations

Measuring success is a critical component in any strategy. The current communication strategy acknowledges the need to measure performance and effectiveness toward achieving the objectives but fails to provide the metrics. Instead, the strategy solicits input from the different departments and agencies, "The PCC will analyze the performance indicators submitted by departments and agencies with a view to approve a uniform set of relevant core indicators for use in all agencies." [24] To facilitate implementation, the authors of the new strategy should provide the metrics and the methodology of obtaining feedback.

13

Means, Observations and Recommendations

The current strategy recognizes that all segments of the United States Government should contribute and recommends three additional structures be established to assist with interagency coordination and meeting the objectives (Counterterrorism Communications Center, Interagency Crisis Communication Team, and regular monitoring of implementation).[25] In addition, the strategy requests that all segments of the United States Government participate by developing an agency-specific plan, sharing information, and scheduling media events.

The new strategy should not only acknowledge and leverage the capabilities of all segments of the United States Government, but it must be more directive in nature and carry the authority of the president. To illustrate this point, consider that the word "should" was used 96 times in the current strategy while the term "will" was used only ten times to define responsibilities. The new administration must recognize that it is not enough to encourage participation; the new document must task the different segments of government to write and implement their own supporting plans. In order to have this tasking authority, the new strategy must be endorsed by the President. A more directive strategy with a presidential endorsement would ensure compliance.

Suitability

The current strategy fails in two regards. Suitability is a common criterion for evaluating a strategy by questioning if accomplishing the stated objectives will produce the desired effect. The first problem with the current strategy is that the attainment of the three stated objectives[26] will not achieve the strategy's desired effect, "...to be a partner for progress, prosperity and peace around the world."[27] The first and third

14

objectives do not mention or imply partnering with other nations.[28] The first objective, "… offer a positive vision of hope and opportunity…" implies activities internal to the United States. The third objective, "America must work to nurture common interests and values…" advocates working to improve relations with other nations but stops short of working together toward a common cause. Although the second objective states that "With our partners, we seek to…" the objective is narrowly focused on the war on terror and in itself cannot achieve the desired effect, "…to be a partner for progress, prosperity and peace around the world."[29]

The second reason the strategy will fail in terms of suitability is that it omits two critical audiences, the "American people" and "traditional friends, coalition partners, and allies." These audiences are critical for achieving the overall success of this strategy. Although not a requirement, a technique of clarifying what objectives apply to which audiences is to include the applicable audience(s) in the stated objective. A revised objective could state that U.S. friends, coalition partners, and allies are reassured of the United State's resolve to honor all commitments.

Finally, to provide greater clarity, the objectives should include the specific audience for which the outcome is desired. The new strategy must be built on a solid framework. As a derivative of the National Security Strategy (NSS), the new *Strategy for Public Diplomacy and Strategic Communication* and like the current strategy, should begin with a vision or end state that directly supports the NSS. Next, the document should provide objectives that when accomplished will produce the desired end state.

Feasibility

All but the most critical of activities can be accomplished using the available means. Feasibility is a criterion for evaluating a strategy by questioning if the action(s) can be accomplished by the available means. The current strategy recognizes that all segments of the United States Government should contribute to the Public Diplomacy and Strategic Communication strategy. There is no doubt that mobilizing and synergizing the efforts of all segments of the United States Government with a common vision would have a profound effect. The problem, however, is that the organization tasked with coordinating these efforts across the interagency community lacks unity of effort, authority, and permanence.

According to the *U.S. National Strategy for Public Diplomacy and Strategic Communication,*

> The Policy Coordinating Committee (PCC) on Public Diplomacy and Strategic Communication led by the Under Secretary for Public Diplomacy and Public Affairs is the overall mechanism by which we coordinate our public diplomacy across the interagency community.[30]

On the surface, this seems to provide a logical solution for coordinating the efforts across the interagency community. However, the Under Secretary for Public Diplomacy and Public Affairs works directly for the Secretary of State. As such, the committee's focus, either intentionally or unintentionally, is on matters important to the secretary of State. The current strategy produced by the PCC overwhelmingly focuses on a war of ideas with violent extremists.

Unity of effort is also degraded by PCC's membership, which according to Christopher Midura's testimony, is limited to "… civilian and military communications leaders from the Departments of State, Defense and the Treasury, the National Security

16

Council, the Intelligence Community, and other agencies."[31] The point is that all other agencies must be included. This view was articulated in the Defense Science Board (DSB) Task Force on Strategic Communication report that recommended, "a permanent strategic communication structure … [with] … a Strategic Communication Policy Committee… to include all departments and agencies with substantial strategic communication responsibilities."[32] Failing to include some agencies increases the risk of an inconsistent message and valuable input they may provide.

The PCC on Public Diplomacy and Strategic Communication is also handicapped by its lack of authority. Although part of the National Security Council (NSC) organizational structure, the PCC is a working group chaired by an Under Secretary and requires its recommendations to pass through the Deputies Committee (DC) before reaching the Principles Committee (PC). With the lack of real authority, the PCC must rely on collaboration and personal relationships.[33] Without the president's endorsement, agencies and departments within the government could choose to ignore the PCC's recommendations.

Finally, the PCC on Public Diplomacy and Strategic Communication is hampered in that it is not a permanent organizational structure. As described in the DSB's report, "Presidents shape the nation's strategic communication in powerful ways, and they require permanent structures within the White House that will strengthen their ability to understand and communicate with global audiences." [34]

In order to establish a feasible *U.S. National Strategy for Public Diplomacy and Strategic Communication* and resolve these problems, the administration must establish a permanent and separate organization with direct access to the president.[35] Authority to implement the communication strategy would come directly from the highest level of government.

Senator Samuel Brownback (R – KS) has taken this recommendation to the next step by sponsoring the Strategic Communications Act of 2008.[36] This bill establishes a National Center for Strategic Communication to advise the President.[37] It would implement the Defense Science Board's recommendation of creating a permanent strategic communication structure and resolving feasibility shortcomings.

Senator Brownback's bill, however, defines strategic communication in such a manner as to limit the scope of the new organization to "foreign audiences."[38] Limiting the scope of this new organization is impractical and incompatible with providing a comprehensive strategy for strategic communication. The bill should be amended to remove "foreign audiences" from the definition of strategic communication. This existing limitation unnecessarily impedes the new recommended organization in developing and implementing a comprehensive strategic communication strategy.

Acceptability

Acceptability is the criterion for evaluating a strategy by questioning if the desired effect is worth the cost. The current strategy recognizes the need for accountability. "Performance measurement and evaluation ensure accountability and transparency so that stakeholders, including the American public, can justify program expenditures as a prudent use of taxpayer funds." However, acceptability of the current strategy is difficult to evaluate. Although the strategy recognizes the need to evaluate its effectiveness, it fails to provide measures of effectiveness and funding to support additional public diplomacy and strategic communication activities.

The current strategy acknowledges the need to evaluate progress by tracking

measures of performance and measures of effectiveness, however, the strategy fails to

provide these metrics. Instead, the strategy solicits input from the different departments

and agencies,

> The PCC will analyze the performance indicators submitted by
> departments and agencies with a view to approve a uniform set of relevant
> core indicators for use in all agencies.[39]

While most U.S. Government agencies already accept the financial burden of

conducting some public diplomacy and strategic communication activities, this strategy

is tasking them to increase their activities, as well as track the results. To accomplish

this mission, additional funding is required. In addition to establishing a permanent

organization for coordinating the nation's public diplomacy and strategic communication

program, Congress should establish a fund controlled by this new organization. Other

government agencies could submit their program strategies for additional funding. This

collaboration would both encourage participation while providing a mechanism for

tracking costs.

Conclusion

With an apparent mismatch between the administration's and most American's

realities and with a new president, the Obama administration will need to reexamine the

U.S. National Strategy for Public Diplomacy and Strategic Communication. This paper

recommended several changes critical to the success of a new strategy. The most

important recommendations consist of establishing a permanent organization for

coordinating the nation's public diplomacy and strategic communication program,

establishing a fund controlled by this new organization, reexamining the strategy's

19

objectives, and expanding the audiences to include friends, coalition partners, allies and the United States domestic audiences. Without these changes, the next administration may also experience a similar mismatch in realities.

Endnotes

[1] George W. Bush, *The National Security Strategy of the United States of America* (Washington, DC: The White House, March 2006), http://www.whitehouse.gov/ nsc/nss/ 2006/nss2006.pdf (accessed November 02, 2008).

[2] BBC World Service, "Global Poll: Majority Wants Troops Out of Iraq Within a Year," September 6, 2007, http://www.worldpublicopinion.org/pipa/pdf/sep07/ BBCIraq_Sep07_rpt.pdf, (accessed December 20, 2008).

[3] "Foreign Policy, Barack Obama and Joe Biden: The Change We Need", http://www.barackobama.com /index.php, (accessed December 14, 2008).

[4] Defense Science Board, *Report of the Defense Science Board Task Force on Strategic Communication* (Washington DC: Office of the Under Secretary of Defense for Acquisition, Technology and Logistics, 2008), 4.

[5] Ibid.

[6] Ibid.

[7] Harry R Yarger, "Toward a Theory of Strategy: Art Lykke and the Army War College Strategy Model, in *U.S. Army War College Guide to National Security Issues, Volume I: Theory of War and Strategy*, ed. J. Boone Bartholomees, Jr. June 2008 (Carlisle, PA: U.S. Army War College, June 2008), 47.

[8] Ibid.

[9] Ibid.

[10] Ibid.

[11] Ibid., 48.

[12] National Security Council Strategic Communication and Public Diplomacy Policy Coordination Committee, *U.S. National Strategy for Public Diplomacy and Strategic Communication* (Washington, DC: The National Security Council, May 2007), 3, http://www.state.gov/documents/organization/87427.pdf, (accessed October 27, 2008).

[13] U.S. Joint Chief of Staff, *Department of Defense Dictionary of Military and Associated Terms*, Joint *Publication 1-02:* (Washington, DC: U.S.. Joint Chiefs of Staff, 2008), 391, http://www.dtic.mil/doctrine/jel/doddict /data/o/03812.html. (accessed December 20, 2008).

[14] This argument goes beyond this paper. In his article, *Towards A Theory of Strategy: Art Lykke and the Army War College Strategy Model,* H. Richard Yarger defines an end state as "what" is to be accomplished and goes on to state that "Ends are expressed with verbs (i.e., deter war, promote regional stability, destroy Iraqi armed forces)." The question is how can the result of an action(s) be described with an activity? This question is for another paper.

[15] USA Today/Gallup Poll, Nov. 7-9 2008, linked from *PollingReport.com Home Page* at "Problems and Priorities", http://www.pollingreport.com/prioriti.htm (accessed December 20, 2008).

[16] German Marshall Fund of the United States and the Compagnia di San Paolo, *Transatlantic Trends 08* (Washington, DC: German Marshall Fund of the United States and the Compagnia di San Paolo, 2008), 6, http://www.transatlantictrends.org/trends/ doc/2008_ English_Key.pdf (accessed December 16, 2008).

[17] Joseph S. Nye, Jr, "The Decline of America's Soft Power," *Foreign Affairs,* 83 no. 3 (May-June 2004), 16-20, In ProQuest.

[18] National Security Council Strategic Communication and Public Diplomacy Policy Coordination Committee, *U.S. National Strategy for Public Diplomacy and Strategic Communication.* 4.

[19] Ibid.

[20] Richard A.Posner, "Bad News", *New York times,* July 31, 2005, http://www.nytimes.com/2005/07/31/books/review/31POSNER.html?_r=3&pagewanted=print (accessed December 14, 2008).

[21] Ibid.

[22] Ibid.

[23] U.S. Joint Forces Command, Joint Warfighting Center, "Established Policy and Guidance" in *Commander's Handbook for Strategic Communication,*(Washington, DC: U.S. Joint Forces Command, September 1, 2008), 12.

[24] National Security Council Strategic Communication and Public Diplomacy Policy Coordination Committee, *U.S. National Strategy for Public Diplomacy and Strategic Communication,* 33.

[25] Ibid., 8.

[26] Ibid., 3. The three stated objectives are: 1) America must offer a positive vision of hope and opportunity that is rooted in our most basic values. 2) With our partners, we seek to isolate and marginalize violent extremists who threaten the freedom and peace sought by civilized people of every nation, culture and faith. 3) America must work to nurture common interests and values between Americans and peoples of different countries, cultures and faiths across the world.

[27] Ibid.

[28] Ibid. Current strategy's stated objectives: 1) America must offer a positive vision of hope and opportunity that is rooted in our most basic values. 2) With our partners, we seek to isolate and marginalize violent extremists who threaten the freedom and peace sought by civilized people of every nation, culture and faith. 3) America must work to nurture common interests and values between Americans and peoples of different countries, cultures and faiths across the world.

[29] Ibid.

[30] Ibid., 8.

[31] Testimony of Christopher Midura, Acting Director, Office of Policy, Planning and Resources Under Secretary for Public Diplomacy and Public Affairs, U.S. Department of State, Before the Senate Homeland Security and Governmental Affairs Subcommittee on Oversight of Government Management, the Federal Workforce, and the District of Columbia September 23, 2008, http://hsgac.senate.gov/public/_files/MiduraTestimony092308.pdf (acessed December 30, 2008)

[32] Defense Science Board, *Report of the Defense Science Board Task Force on Strategic Communication*, 94.

[33] Alan G. Whittaker, Frederick C. Smith, & Elizabeth McKune, *The National Security Policy Process: The National Security Council and Interagency System.* Research Report, (Washington, DC: Industrial College of the Armed Forces, National Defense University, U.S. Department of Defense, April 2007), 27.

[34] Defense Science Board, *Report of the Defense Science Board Task Force on Strategic Communication*, xiii.

[35] Ibid., xv.

[36] This is the third bill introduced. Two earlier bills included, the Strategic Communication Act of 2007 and the Strategic Communication Act of 2005 both sponsored by U.S. Representative William (Mac) Thornberry (Texas).

[37] Senator Samuel Brownback (Kansas), *Strategic Communications Act of 2008*, S 3546 IS 110th CONGRESS 2d Session, September 23 (legislative day, September 17), 2008 linked from GovTrack.us, http://www.govtrack.us/congress/bill.xpd?bill=s110-3546 (accessed December 21, 2008).

[38] Ibid.

[39] National Security Council Strategic Communication and Public Diplomacy Policy Coordination Committee, *U.S. National Strategy for Public Diplomacy and Strategic Communication,* 33.